Sway in the Wind-blown Branches with
ORANGUTANS

D1533716

Published by Wildlife Education, Ltd.
12233 Thatcher Court, Poway, California 92064
contact us at: **1-800-477-5034**
e-mail us at: **animals@zoobooks.com**
visit us at: **www.zoobooks.com**

ISBN 0-937934-83-6

Orangutans

Series Created by
John Bonnett Wexo

Written by
John Bonnett Wexo
Marjorie Betts Shaw

Scientific Consultants
Charles A. McLaughlin, Ph.D.

Mark Rich, M.S.

Contents

BORNEAN MALE, OVER 15 YEARS OLD

3 TO 4 YEARS OLD

SUMATRAN MALE,
OVER 15 YEARS OLD

5 TO 7 YEARS OLD

Orangutans live in the trees of the rain forest on the tropical islands of Sumatra and Borneo. Sumatra and most of Borneo belong to Indonesia. In the Indonesian language, orangutan means "person of the forest." Because they spend most of their lives in the trees, orangs are often hard to see as they travel through dense foliage high above the ground. The Dayak peoples of Borneo have a legend that orangutans are really ghosts that can suddenly appear or disappear.

Orangutans, gorillas, and chimpanzees are all great apes. Although orangs are smaller than gorillas, they are very large for animals that are tree dwellers. Males can be 4½ feet tall and have great strength. In the wild, they usually weigh about 160 pounds. The much smaller females weigh about 80 pounds. In zoos, where food is more plentiful, males sometimes weigh more than 350 pounds!

There are two different kinds of orangutans, and they are quite different in appearance. On Borneo, orangs tend to be heavyset, with coarse,

7 TO 9 YEARS OLD

BORNEAN FEMALE,
OVER 9 YEARS OLD

6 TO 12 MONTHS OLD

4 TO 6 YEARS OLD

BORNEAN MALE
OVER 12 YEARS OLD

orange-red hair and dark-gray skin. The hair is usually long on their shoulders and back—sometimes more than a foot long. Males of the Bornean orangutan develop huge cheek flaps and throat pouches as they grow older.

Sumatran orangs are taller, more slender, and have narrower faces than Bornean orangs. Their long hair is a lighter red, and the males grow long, flowing mustaches and beards that make them look like wise old men. This look is not deceiving, because orangutans are highly intelligent animals.

Scientists believe that they are among the most intelligent of all land animals. They use sticks as tools in their search for food. The observational skills they use for finding the best fruiting trees in the forest help them find the best way out of their enclosures in captivity! In zoos, orangutans are known as "escape artists" that can confound the best architects, builders, and keepers.

In the wild, orangutans may live to be more than 40 years old. In zoos, where medical care is available, they may live an additional 15 to 20 years.

7

Without any hair, the orangs in this illustration might remind you of "the man on the flying trapeze," but when it comes to body build and movement, humans and orangutans are exact opposites.

An orangutan's long arms, mobile shoulders, and strong upper muscles let the orang use its arms to "walk" through the forest. The orangutan's weight is supported by its arms and shoulders. A human's weight is supported by its long, strong legs.

Orangutans are superbly adapted for life in the trees. For most of them, the leafy canopy of the tropical forest provides everything they need in life, and they rarely descend to the forest floor. One reason for the high life of an orangutan is safety. In the upper levels of the forest, they have no natural enemies. At night, when predators prowl below, orangutans sleep soundly in nests as much as 70 feet above the ground.

As they swing from tree to tree, the only danger orangutans face is the possibility of a bone-breaking fall. Although the swing of an orang seems effortless, its path is carefully chosen and tested for supportability. The way orangs move through the trees is called brachiation. They hook their long fingers over a branch or vine and swing forward, grasping the next branch with the other hand. In this manner they continue to travel hand over hand.

Such swinging seems easy and natural, but baby orangs do not automatically know how to brachiate. Their mothers must teach them. An

An orangutan's arms are 1½ times longer than its legs. The arms are also much stronger than the legs.

Stretch your arms as far as you can and have someone measure the length of your reach. An orangutan's reach can measure as much as eight feet from fingertip to fingertip! And those long arms can swing in all directions.

The orangutan's short flexible legs and long flexible feet can also be used for swinging through the trees. They are not so useful for walking on the ground.

adult orang's body hangs straight down as it swings through the forest. A young orang is not as secure in its ability and often holds onto a vine with its feet while it reaches for a branch with its hands.

Once the skill is developed, young orangs become active and daring. They swing in the highest branches and scamper to the tops of the tallest trees to look around for food and to choose the best route through the forest canopy. If an aggressive adult male tries to chase them away, young orangs choose escape routes with

branches and vines they know are too delicate to support the adult's weight. As orangs grow older and heavier, their caution increases.

On the ground, orangutans' long arms get in the way, and their short legs have trouble supporting the weight of their bodies. The arms are either used like crutches—planting them on the ground and swinging between them—or held in the air for balance as they waddle along. Not surprisingly, orangutans go to great lengths to find a tree route when they want to go anywhere.

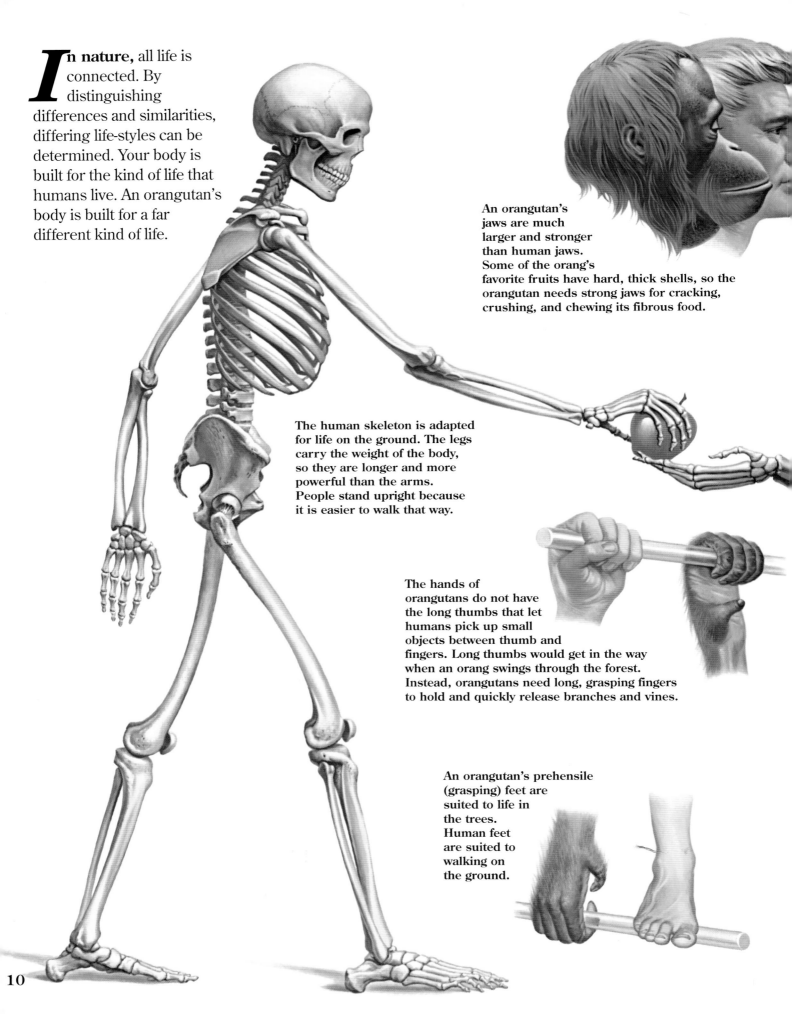

*I*n nature, all life is connected. By distinguishing differences and similarities, differing life-styles can be determined. Your body is built for the kind of life that humans live. An orangutan's body is built for a far different kind of life.

An orangutan's jaws are much larger and stronger than human jaws. Some of the orang's favorite fruits have hard, thick shells, so the orangutan needs strong jaws for cracking, crushing, and chewing its fibrous food.

The human skeleton is adapted for life on the ground. The legs carry the weight of the body, so they are longer and more powerful than the arms. People stand upright because it is easier to walk that way.

The hands of orangutans do not have the long thumbs that let humans pick up small objects between thumb and fingers. Long thumbs would get in the way when an orang swings through the forest. Instead, orangutans need long, grasping fingers to hold and quickly release branches and vines.

An orangutan's prehensile (grasping) feet are suited to life in the trees. Human feet are suited to walking on the ground.

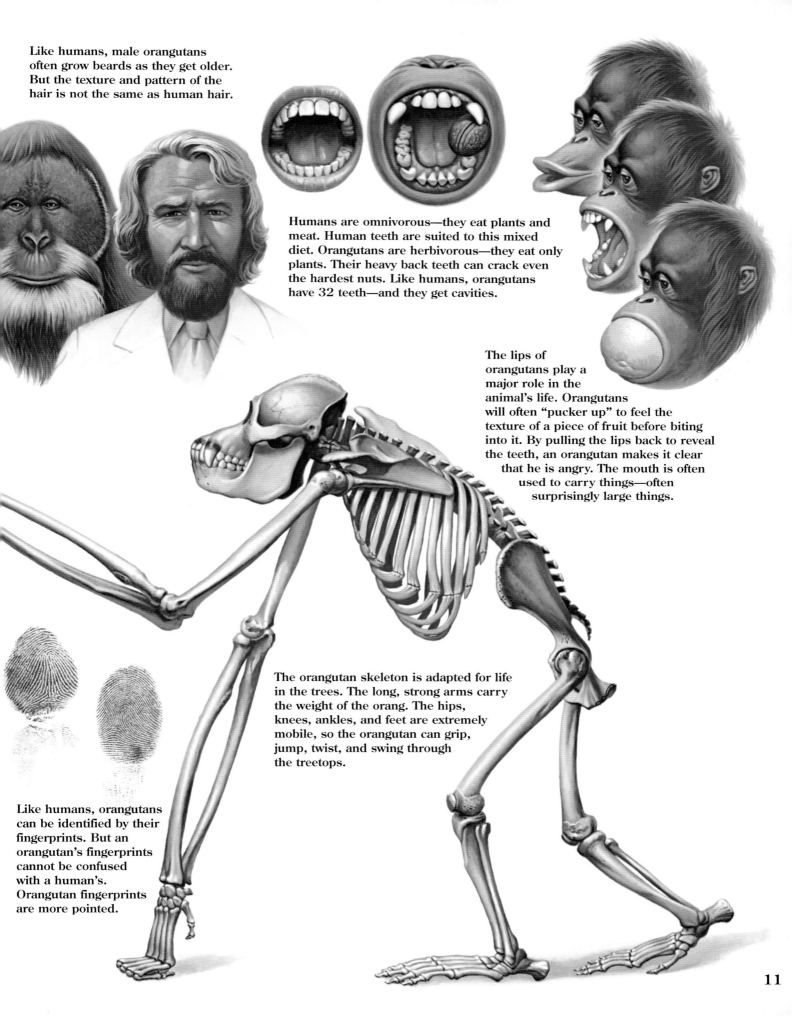

Like humans, male orangutans often grow beards as they get older. But the texture and pattern of the hair is not the same as human hair.

Humans are omnivorous—they eat plants and meat. Human teeth are suited to this mixed diet. Orangutans are herbivorous—they eat only plants. Their heavy back teeth can crack even the hardest nuts. Like humans, orangutans have 32 teeth—and they get cavities.

The lips of orangutans play a major role in the animal's life. Orangutans will often "pucker up" to feel the texture of a piece of fruit before biting into it. By pulling the lips back to reveal the teeth, an orangutan makes it clear that he is angry. The mouth is often used to carry things—often surprisingly large things.

The orangutan skeleton is adapted for life in the trees. The long, strong arms carry the weight of the orang. The hips, knees, ankles, and feet are extremely mobile, so the orangutan can grip, jump, twist, and swing through the treetops.

Like humans, orangutans can be identified by their fingerprints. But an orangutan's fingerprints cannot be confused with a human's. Orangutan fingerprints are more pointed.

11

Food is the consuming passion of an orangutan's life. Every hour that an orang is awake, it is more likely to be searching for food than to be doing anything else.

Wild orangutans eat more than 300 kinds of foods. They are the largest-bodied fruit eaters on earth. From April to November of each year, many different fruits ripen. The orangutans eat heavily during this period to store fat and energy for the lean months ahead. During the rest of the year, when fruit is scarce, they eat leaves, bark, the tree layers immediately beneath the bark, and some grasses.

The social structure of orangs in the forest is affected by the location and number of food sources. Fruit trees are usually widely separated, and there is rarely enough fruit on a single tree for more than one or two orangs to eat. So the solitary life of the orang helps it to survive. Male orangutans travel alone, and females are usually accompanied by only one or two of their own children.

Ants, termites, crickets, caterpillars, and honey are also consumed. An orang will sometimes use a tool to get these delicacies. It breaks a stick to a convenient length and holds it in its mouth. Then, grasping the tree tightly, it pounds the stick into a termite nest, an ant nest, or a nest with honey, and dines on what it finds. Sticks are also used to remove the prickly spines from a favorite fruit before it is eaten.

In captivity it appears that orangutans like to decorate themselves with their food. In the wild they show similar behavior by draping leaves, twigs, and branches over themselves as protection from rainfall, too much sun, or even from biting and stinging insects. What looks like an orangutan's "hat" may actually be its "umbrella."

Young orangs are not adept at eating some of the spiny fruits, like the durian, that the adults eat. They must learn how to remove the spines before they can enjoy the fruit. Bananas, of course, are easier to get into.

JACKFRUIT

DURIAN

LANGSAT

BREADFRUIT, OR PANDANUS

WILD PLUM

MANGOSTEEN

PITH OF WADAN,
OR CLIMBING
BAMBOO

RAMBUTAN

STRANGLER FIG

***T**he orangutan's solitary life* is unique among the great apes. Gorillas and chimpanzees live in large groups that eat and travel together. But a mother and her offspring are the orangutan family unit.

A young orang stays with its mother until she has another baby. By this time, the first offspring is between 6 and 10 years old. A female may not give birth until the age of 15. Because females keep their young with them for many years, they may have only two or three offspring during their lifetimes.

Adult males tolerate females and sometimes stay with a female for 20 days or more during courtship and mating, but they are aggressive toward other males and avoid contact except to fight.

Female orangutans are attentive, affectionate parents. This mother will keep contact with her youngster for up to ten years.

Orangutans that have large, overlapping home ranges recognize their neighbors when they meet—perhaps in a fruit tree—but there is limited interaction. Adult females are friendly with females of all ages and accept the presence of males, but tend to forage only with their most recent offspring.

When a mature male is ready to mate, he bellows loudly and sometimes breaks branches and flings them to the ground. This attracts females that are ready to mate, but sends mothers with young fleeing to the treetops. Less mature males in the area usually retreat.

By far the most sociable among the orangutans are the juveniles and adolescents, who play and sometimes travel together.

*L*ife in the forest means life in the trees for an orangutan. In the wild, they seldom come to the ground. They eat, sleep, and mate in the trees. And when they want to travel, they travel through the trees, high off the forest floor. When a favorite tree bears fruit, an orang might spend the day gorging itself on its favorite diet.

Young orangs spend a lot of time together—playing, eating, and investigating their surroundings. Sometimes they inspect a friend's meal in progress!

Orangutans build nests to sleep in the trees and sometimes cover themselves to keep warm and dry. An infant orang shares the nest with its mother. As a youngster grows older, it may build its own nest very near its mother's nest.

Compare the hands here and you will see that the hands of orangutans, with their very long fingers and short thumbs, are better able to hook over branches and vines on their aerial pathways through the forest.

ORANGUTAN CHIMPANZEE HUMAN GORILLA

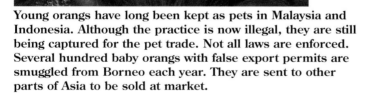

Young orangs have long been kept as pets in Malaysia and Indonesia. Although the practice is now illegal, they are still being captured for the pet trade. Not all laws are enforced. Several hundred baby orangs with false export permits are smuggled from Borneo each year. They are sent to other parts of Asia to be sold at market.

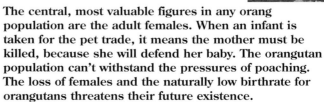

The central, most valuable figures in any orang population are the adult females. When an infant is taken for the pet trade, it means the mother must be killed, because she will defend her baby. The orangutan population can't withstand the pressures of poaching. The loss of females and the naturally low birthrate for orangutans threatens their future existence.

The orangutan's future is tied to the future of the rain forest. But much of the forest is being logged for timber or cleared for agriculture and large plantations. Suitable habitat for orangutans declined by more than 80 percent between 1973 and 1993. And the number of orangutans has decreased by 30 to 50 percent since 1985.

On Sumatra, an estimated 9,200 orangutans live in and around a national park at the far north of the island. Wildlife biologists hope that the park will be enlarged to include more low, swampy land, which is good habitat for orangs. They also want a corridor of forest restored that will connect the separated populations. If these habitat improvements are made, the Sumatran orangs may be able to increase their numbers. Now is a critical time. For long-term survival, their numbers should not drop below 10,000.

On Borneo, there are 10,000 to 15,500 orangutans, but they are divided between several isolated populations. Sixty percent of the Bornean orangutans can be protected just by enforcing current laws.

Fragmentation of habitat and poaching continue to threaten the orangutan's existence. By protecting the orangutan and its habitat, many other rain forest animals and plants will be saved as well.

There has been some success in returning young captive orangutans to the wild. These orangs must first be trained to live in the forest. They cannot be released into a wild population, because they might carry disease to wild orangs. But they can be released into areas *formerly* occupied by wild orangutans.

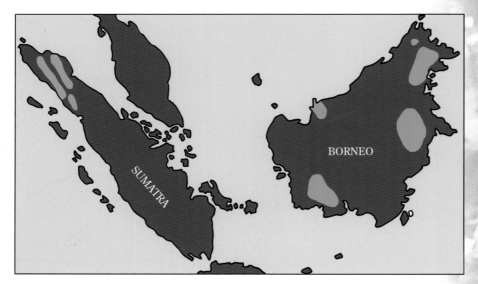

Index